CAMERACOLOUR PORTRAIT

The
South Pennines
and the
Brontë Country

Photographs by SIMON WARNER
Text by JUDITH and SIMON WARNER

Town County BOOKS

A Member of the Ian Allan Group of Companies

First published 1984

ISBN 0 86364 018 4

Photographs © Simon Warner

© Town & County Books Ltd 1984

Published by Town & County Books Ltd, Shepperton, Surrey;
and printed by Ian Allan Printing
at their works at Coombelands, Runnymede, England

INTRODUCTION

A double-headed Christmas Special leaving Haworth station on the Worth Valley Railway.

The name 'South Pennines', coined somewhat inaccurately in the early 1970s for an area that is strictly speaking at the centre of the north-south Pennine chain, suggests more cohesion for this part of England than perhaps exists. Plans were made in 1973 with the idea of establishing a Regional Recreation Area over this rather amorphous region, half in Lancashire and half in Yorkshire, and the 'official' name of South Pennines was conjured up to cover it. A cursory glance at the map of the area leaves one largely unsurprised that the new 'Park' never came into existence. Apart from the fact that it straddles the boundary of two remote corners of two different counties, it is beseiged by cities whose names have been a byword for the worst excesses of the Industrial Revolution — Leeds, Bradford, Burnley, Rochdale, Oldham, Huddersfield, Halifax — to name but a few. The map also shows an area pockmarked with reservoirs — whose extensive catchment areas are the subject of stringent restriction upon both residents and visitors. Furthermore, the region is not large, and yet one end is lopped off by the M62 which cuts remorselessly across the moors south of Blackstone Edge, slicing through the Pennine Way — the modern ramblers' sacred path — like a knife. The landscape remaining, as seen on the map, appears to be an uneasy juxtaposition of overpopulated valleys lying in the backwash of industrial progress, and empty moorland which nowhere appears to contort itself into features that might bear the name 'mountainous'. Lastly, the South Pennines are sandwiched rather ignominiously between those two great National Parks, the Yorkshire Dales and the Peak District. To these Parks' undoubted claims for variety, grandeur and unspoiled rural calm, the South Pennines may seem to offer only a Cinderella-like resignation, sitting as they do in the ashes of the dying industrial furnace

Lothersdale, a remote mill village in the north of the region near Skipton, with a unique mixture of millstone grit and limestone rocks.

which forged much of what they are today. But there is, as this book reveals, a great deal more to the region than immediately meets the eye.

The South Pennines' main claim to cohesion, and its main difference from its regal sisters to the north and south, lies under the surface, in the composition of the rock itself. It is here that the true shape of the region was generated, and here that the apparently wayward forces of history were in fact dictated and channelled. It is as though the rock itself carried a genetic code which shaped the landscape, determined the vegetation, and established the character of the people who lived on it and the uses to which they put the land.

The rock which stretches for 30 miles or so from the Aire Gap south of Skipton to the Derbyshire border is not the white porous limestone of Malham in the Dales or Dovedale in the Peak District. It is the darker, harder Millstone Grit, which gives the build-ing stone its characteristic black appearance when exposed, and which creates a profusion of moorland steams and rivers on its water-resistant surface. The smooth undulating moors, creased with infolding valleys, and marked frequently by rock outcroppings, give the appearance of dour ruggedness which belies their vulnerability to almost every exploitation man has conceived of: water catchment, coal mining, quarrying, the construction of trans-Pennine routes, and every manner of industrial development since the idea of commerce took hold of civilisation and propelled it into this century.

But the routes, the buildings and the features of South Pennines are rooted deeper in history than the present century. Packhorse ways, for example, reach back into the remote past, and are better preserved here than in almost any other region of

Haworth Moor, with Scar Hill and fallen stone walls under a looming sky.

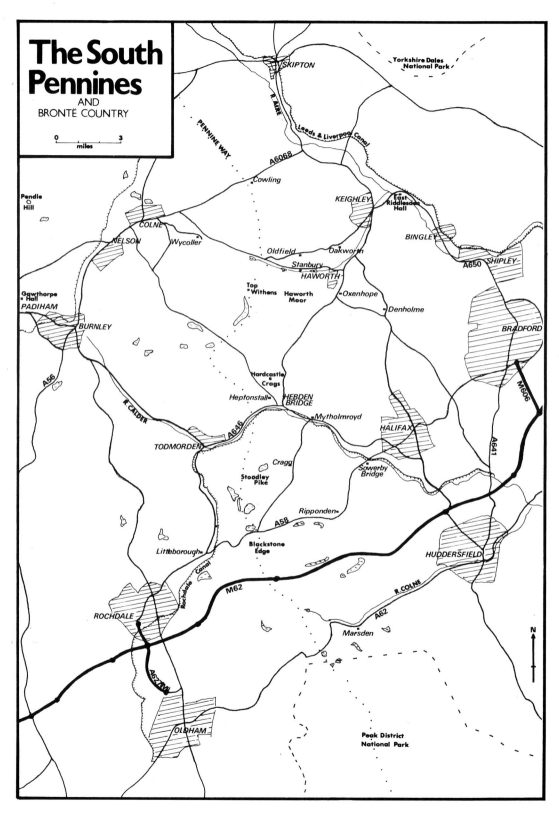

The South Pennines
AND BRONTË COUNTRY

0 — miles — 3

Yorkshire Dales National Park

SKIPTON

R. AIRE

Leeds & Liverpool Canal

PENNINE WAY

A6068

Cowling

Pendle Hill

KEIGHLEY

East Riddlesden Hall

COLNE

BINGLEY

NELSON

Wycoller

Oldfield

Oakworth

A650

SHIPLEY

Stanbury

HAWORTH

Top Withens

Haworth Moor

Oxenhope

Gawthorpe Hall

PADIHAM

Denholme

BURNLEY

BRADFORD

A56

R. CALDER

Hardcastle Crags

Heptonstall

HEBDEN BRIDGE

A646

Mytholmroyd

HALIFAX

M606

TODMORDEN

Cragg

Sowerby Bridge

A641

Stoodley Pike

Ripponden

A58

Blackstone Edge

Littleborough

HUDDERSFIELD

Rochdale Canal

R. COLNE

M62

A62

ROCHDALE

Marsden

N

A627(M)

Peak District National Park

OLDHAM

Wesley's octagonal Methodist Church at Heptonstall.

Britain. Commerce may have created the need for these lines of communication, but it was the landscape that dictated where they should run and how they were constructed, and it is that same landscape that in more recent times has shielded many stretches of ancient way from destruction. Some have disappeared beneath reservoirs, others have been swallowed into roads but many remain, abandoned on moortops or tucked into valleys, left because they were remote and of no more use — priceless examples of our heritage conserved almost by default.

Such routes were always the arteries of a region as disjointed as this. In the days when the valleys were heavily wooded and marshy, isolated dwellings or small communities clung to the sides of the moors, on the springline, taking advantage of the water supply and the best of a fairly poor provision of arable land. The paths linking these old communities and farms are perhaps the oldest ways, often developed through various stages, until modern roads were built in the now drained, treeless valleys, and the moor

tracks were left to sheep and vegetation, or to ramblers. One such route runs intermittently along the north watershed of Haworth Moor, from Pendle Hill in Lancashire across the border and up to the village of Oxenhope, a little southwest of Haworth. The local authority is at present attempting to reopen a stretch of this route as a so-called 'Brontë Corridor' from Haworth to the old weaving hamlet of Wycoller, whose Hall is the supposed inspiration for Ferndean Manor in Charlotte Brontë's *Jane Eyre*. Local historians however know the route to have a history far older and more subtle than anything accessible to adoption by the partial interests of tourism. The route has been called 'The Witch Corridor.' Farms linked by it that have escaped dereliction have revealed, on restoration, the mummified corpses of birds, animals and reptiles set in the thick dry-stone walls. Loops of long-dead and dried rowan are bound round beams that go back centuries, and witch-stones with holes

7

or hollows are a common find. The fame of the persecuted witches of Pendle, tried and largely exterminated by belligerent and prejudiced authority at the beginning of the 17th century is a single episode in the experiences of a past that is enshrined in such ancient buildings as these farms, and by the paths that link them. Most of the details are lost to memory — we are left with these irreplaceable marks on the landscape to preserve such fragments of our past.

When textiles became the single most important commodity in the land the inhabitants of these upland farms modified their way of life and their homes to accommodate the domestic production of cloth. Evidence of such changes are still visible in the architecture of many houses of this period and in the further development of linking trackways to carry the heavy traffic of packhorses. With the coming of the industrial revolution cloth making ceased to be a cottage industry. Many of the industrious and by now quite large population moved down from the moors to the valley mills, and new communities grew, first where the stream waters were strongest up tributary valleys and finally squarely on the wider valley bottoms where roads, canals, and eventually railways supplied the ever-growing factories with fuel and raw materials. Behind this new industrial heartland lay the hill farms, suddenly rural again, often ruined and derelict, and the upper valleys, once silent habitats for the local legends of witchcraft and fairyfolk, were now haunted by a new desolation. Now too, abandoned mills, like graceful castles of imagination succumbing

Halifax, a large industrial town set in a bowl of hills.

8

Eastergate Bridge at the foot of Marsden Moor. From here a medieval packhorse route leads over the Pennines to Rochdale.

beautifully to nature and decay, are themselves it seems, full of the ghosts of an earlier industrial age.

Not that the ghosts of the Pennines fit comfortably into sentimental nostalgia — the landscape's driving spirit is not in the end one of decay, but of a dogged permanence which is always ready to return and absorb man's temporary manipulations. Much of the attraction of this countryside is that no amount of intensive occupation, no amount of effort on the part of builders and engineers who wrestle always with the intractable elements of geology and weather, no amount of council development or tourist erosion seems to tame it into submission. There is about the South Pennines something incalculable in human terms, something that is at once enigmatic and unique, and something infinitely worthy of preservation. Its riches are intact almost because, rather than in spite of, the assaults made upon it in the name of civilisation and progress.

We do not have to move far from the line of the 'Witch Corridor' to arrive at Haworth, the centre of interest for many visitors to the area, and one of the major factors, one presumes, that inspired the concept of a South Pennine Recreation Area. Haworth, once home of the Brontës, is the scene of a story too widely told to need repetition here. This particular book is more concerned with the landscape and its action upon the minds of the artists who experienced it in all seasons, weathers and moods. The mystery of this creative chemistry cannot be precisely defined, only speculated upon. One can reflect, for example, on whether Emily Brontë would have written a novel such as *Wuthering Heights* had she been resident, say, in Hampstead or Penzance or even — to be less frivolous, in Thornton, a few miles nearer to Bradford, where she was born. When looking at her work and life it becomes impossible to ignore how intimate her poetry is with the smallest detail of her immediate landscape. A genius she certainly was, probably a genius born, but the shape her inspiration took was everywhere moulded by these particular moors. The innate qualities she brought to this area were reflected back to her a

Abel Cross, ancient way-markers on the old road from Heptonstall to Haworth.

thousandfold; separated from it she grew physically ill and spiritually arid. Emily conducted what amounted to a deep love affair with Haworth Moor, with its every dip, rise, outcrop, bird and sprig of heather. A mystic she might have been, wherever she might have lived, but her mysticism as it has come down to us in her work grew here, was rooted here, and acknowledged no other force comparable to that of this place. Her salutation to it positively thunders on our ears, over more than a hundred years of time and change:

I'll walk where my own nature would be
  leading:
It vexes me to choose another guide:
Where the gray flocks in ferny glens are
  feeding,
Where the wild wind blows on the
  mountain side.

What have these lonely mountains worth
  revealing?
More glory and more grief than I can
  tell:
The earth that wakes one *human heart to*
  feeling
Can centre both the worlds of Heaven
  and Hell.

Emily Brontë, from *Stanzas*

As Winifred Gérin observed in her biography, Emily absorbed the landscape into the act of creation: no book is less rewarding than *Wuthering Heights* for the superficial shrine-hunter who treks the moors in search of definite locations, yet few books are more rewarding for a visitor who has felt, on his or her own account, the dramatic power inherent in the place as a whole:

'She knew the places so well that she never troubled to describe them for her readers, other than by passing allusions. It was the Tudor farmstead up at Top Withins where she had known the "stunted row of firs at the end of the house", "the gaunt thorns stretching their limbs one way, as though craving alms of the sun". It was the year "1801" carved over the porch of Ponden House that dated the climax of the drama for her; and the interior of Ponden, so often visited in girlhood, with its high mantelpieces and oak beams, that furnished the homes of the Lintons and Earnshaws. Without the exact relative positions of Ponden to Withins, the four miles separating Thrushcross Grange from Wuthering Heights would not have been so essential a topographical detail in the lives of the two households. Without the hollow rock towering at the head of the Ponden Valley, with its passage below and the local legends attaching to it, there would have been no "fairy cave under Penistone Crag" or "witches gathering elf-locks to hurt heifers" in *Wuthering Heights*. No book was more rooted in its native soil, more conditioned by the local background of its author, than *Wuthering Heights*.'

Winifred Gérin: *Emily Brontë*

It is easy enough to claim a unique personality for this area — but less easy to say precisely how this singularity can be defined. The South Pennines are most certainly not picturesque; it is a much scarred district, one that 20 years ago was in a severe decline which halted only with the new growth of tourism and the arrival of commuters from the neighbouring major cities seeking out country homes at a reasonable price. Industry, transport, agriculture, tourism and the water authorities have all had their varying slices out of the region but even those places that have, to a large extent, remained 'wild', beyond the roads, buildings, reservoirs, and designated footpaths, where there is only grass and rock, heather and grouse, a treacherous expanse of bog and a rewarding sense of silence — even this little that is left is, so far as the beautiful goes, at best an acquired taste. That is, if we are to believe some of the visitors and residents of the past.

Mrs Gaskell's comments following her first visit to Haworth and its environs have coloured feelings about it ever since:

'All around the horizon there is this same line of sinuous wave-like hills; the scoops into which they fall only revealing other hills beyond, of similar colour and shape, crowned with wild, bleak moors — grand, from the ideas of solitude and loneliness which they suggest; or oppressive from the feeling which they give of being pent-up by some monotonous and illimitable barrier, according to the mood of mind in which the spectator may be.'

Elizabeth Gaskell,
The Life of Charlotte Brontë

These are fair, if partial, comments from a woman who had made her home in a city, and who busied herself with the social concerns of her age. Charlotte herself seems to have held the same opinions. Often prone to writing apologias for Emily, she did the like for her moorland landscape. It must never be assumed that the Brontës as a family enjoyed banishment to such a place — they were outsiders in their village of adoption, Celtic in origin like both their parents and as foreign, perhaps, to the real Yorkshire type as that supposed Yorkshire devil-incarnate — Heathcliff. He was probably an orphan of the Irish famine, picked up as he was in Liverpool docks like a stray cat. Charlotte's maternal aunt mourned her native Cornwall all her life; the youngest sister, Anne, chose to die and be buried near her beloved sea, at Scarborough. Charlotte herself seems less than ecstatic about these moors:

'The scenery of these hills is not grand — it is not romantic; it is scarcely striking. Long, low moors, dark with heath, shut in little valleys, where a stream waters, here and there, a fringe of stunted copse. Mills and scattered cottages chase romance from these valleys; it is only higher up, deep in amongst the ridges of the moors, that Imagination can find rest for the sole of her foot.'

Charlotte Brontë:
Memoir of Emily Brontë in *Poems*.

Here she is speaking, for once, like a true product of her age. The 'romance' which she finds so lacking seems less akin to Emily's art than to the poetry of Wordsworth, obsessed as he was with the concept of a romantic rural innocence which pre-dated the evils of

Holmfirth, a tightly-knit small town in the Holme Valley south of Huddersfield.

12

industrialisation. To Charlotte's eyes, and the eyes of any Victorian artist seeking the picturesque, the land was either despoiled or barren. Yet she does make another point in the same essay, one which moves nearer to the perception Emily had of the moors, but it is a grudging shift: Imagination, she says,

'if she demand beauty to inspire her... must bring it inborn: these moors are too stern to yield any product so delicate. The eye of the gazer must itself brim with a "purple light".... Unless that light and freshness are innate and self-sustained, the drear prospect of a Yorkshire moor will be found as barren of poetic as of agricultural interest.'

(ibid)

Emily differs in that she invests the land itself with a spirit at least equal to her own and, in her words quoted earlier, states a claim for this spirit of place unparalleled in our literature. The English have always remained coy where their mystical roots are concerned. Catherine in *Wuthering Heights* surely speaks for her creator when she dreams she is in heaven, and weeps to go home:

'and the angels were so angry that they flung me out into the middle of the heath on the top of Wuthering Heights; where I woke sobbing for joy.'

Wuthering Heights is eminently a universal novel — yet another paradox which Emily shares with her moors: against a background so timeless and yet so intimately known by the human spirit, clearer truths about the human condition can gleam, unobserved by the brighter lights of any particular age or fashion.

The South Pennines have always attracted tourists, and many of them have been artists, or some species of creatures of the spirit. For so northerly and, we are often told, culturally bereft a place, a surprising number of events have occurred here which have affected the fate of nations. George Fox first experienced the revelations of his new faith on Pendle Hill, and went on to found Quakerism. Nonconformist minds have always stirred an echo in the independently-minded people of Yorkshire. The Wesleys were highly successful in their preaching here. The ministry of William Grimshaw in Haworth which preceded by some years that of Patrick Brontë reached apocryphal heights. And as for Fox — the little village of Stanbury lost many of its inhabitants to the colonies in the 17th century where they went to start new lives, free to worship as they wished. Friends that remained still lie buried in one of England's first Quaker graveyards. It is now a grass plot marked by a simple stone — such a plain testimony to events of great historical importance.

John Wesley visited the area over twenty times, drawn he claimed in his writings, by the unique beauty he, at least, found in a landscape which seemed to answer the spirit of an energetic and freethinking man. Of the Calder Valley, south of Haworth, he wrote that there was not 'anything more delightful than the steep mountains, clothed with wood to the top, and washed at the bottom by a clear, winding stream'. For him, it seemed comparable to Eden.

William Cobbett wrote in *Rural Rides*, in the 1830s, 'This part of England is the most interesting that I ever saw.' Defoe, in his *Tour through the Whole Island of Great Britain* remarked on the densely populated nature of the land, the people 'all full of business' and went on:

'The wildest part of the country is full of variety, the most mountainous places have their rarities to oblige the curious, and give constant employ to the enquiries of a diligent observer.'

With this we agree, without qualification. The land here has a special resonance which the photographs that follow are an attempt to locate and explore. The discovery of the unique spirit of place must of necessity in the end be a personal one — each detail though, is irreplaceable and should be recorded and cherished for the sake of our own well-being.

Judith Warner
Stanbury, West Yorkshire
1984

Ponden Hall, Stanbury, with mounting block.

Leeshaw Reservoir, Oxenhope, West Yorkshire. A typical view from the edge of gritstone moorland. In the centre of the picture is Leeshaw Reservoir which gathers water running off Haworth and Cock Hill Moors. The dark winter colours of Haworth Moor can be seen at the top left while in the distance lies Rombalds Moor on the far side of the Aire Valley. Beyond that are the Dales. The abrupt line of the immediate moorland clearly shows the altitude above which it was uneconomic to 'take in' land for cultivation. The view is from Stairs Lane on the old road from Heptonstall to Haworth which still exists as a footpath and goes over the moor top appropriately enough at Top o' Stairs. From there a more gentle track leads down into Crimsworth Dean. A long circular walk is possible from Haworth using the Pennine Way for the return journey.

Lumb Bridge and Falls, Crimsworth Dean, West Yorkshire. Crimsworth Beck, a tributary of the Calder, runs off Cock Hill Moor down Crimsworth Dean into Hardcastle Crags, at which point it is spanned by this fine packhorse bridge. The survival of so many of these bridges and the paved tracks which crossed them is one of the delights of the South Pennines. This particular route over Lumb Bridge is part of the Limers' Gate ('gate' meaning Way) from limestone deposits near Wycoller to Halifax. It would have been heavily used during the 17th and 18th centuries when lime became popular for improving acid soils. Most packhorse bridges were built without parapets to accommodate the wide packhorse loads; the iron fence here is for the safety of modern pedestrians. The waterfall has been formed by the collapse of a hard gritstone cap which covered softer, more easily eroded shales beneath.

Gibson Mill, Hardcastle Crags, West Yorkshire. Hardcastle Crags Nature Reserve, which now belongs to the National Trust, has long been one of Yorkshire's best loved beauty spots. At one time there were mass outings here from the industrial towns in the valley on Bank Holidays. Lying unexpectedly at its heart, beside the Hebden Water and among beech trees, is this early water-driven cotton mill, built about 1800. The picture also shows one of two large dams in which water from the river was stored. A steam engine was installed in 1852 but was only used when the water supply dried up. The mill was closed at the end of the last century since when the building has been used as a restaurant, and for roller-skating, although it is currently empty. The picturesque location is typical of the South Pennines; every tributary valley has its remains of chimneys, mills and water courses slowly subsiding beneath the natural regeneration. The rural water-powered mills were a first stage of industrialisation. With the advent of steam, industry became concentrated in the main valleys where canal and railway could supply fuel and materials direct to the door.

Hepstonstall Village across Hebden Dale, West Yorkshire. Heptonstall is the gem of Pennine hill villages, perched high on a promontory above the Calder Valley. Site of a Civil War battle in 1643, the village was a very busy settlement in pre-industrial times. It possessed the first Cloth Hall in the Pennines, open as early as 1545. With the introduction of machinery into textile manufacture economic life moved down into the valleys and Heptonstall was preserved from further development as a model weaving village with much fine vernacular architecture from the 17th century. The prominent 19th century church was built alongside the former 15th century building whose tower still stands and can be seen in the picture. Also in Heptonstall is the oldest Methodist chapel in continuous use, designed by John Wesley to an octagonal shape. This view of the village from the north-east shows snow-covered moors rising on the south side of Upper Calderdale.

Hebden Bridge, West Yorkshire
As its name suggests, Hebden
Bridge's original importance was
as a crossing place. Steep tracks
converged on the medieval
bridge across the Hebden Water,
taking packhorse trains from
Heptonstall and beyond to
Halifax. The town of Hebden
Bridge is almost entirely a
creation of the industrial
revolution in the 18th century,
when the concentration of textile
production into large mills in the
valley bottoms established the
lowlands as the main points for
settlement. The precipitous sides
of the Calder Valley and its
Hebden tributary created a
particularly dense concentration
of dwellings in Hebden Bridge.
With level building land at a
premium, a solution was found in
the construction of 'Top and
Bottom Houses' as seen in the
terraces on this hillside. Each
four-storey house was divided
into two two-storey homes, the
upper one having its access from
the higher ground level at the
back. The five-storey Nutclough
Mill, in the upper left quarter of
the picture, was the premises of
an early co-operative of
manufacturers of fustian, a thick
cotton cloth. It has now been
bought and renovated by Pennine
Heritage for re-use by small-scale
industrial enterprises who will
share centralised business
services within the building, an
experiment in partnership in
keeping with the spirit of the
mill's foundation.

24

Greenwood Lee, Heptonstall, West Yorkshire. On a site that has been occupied since early times, this former merchant clothier's house dated 1712 is among the best of many fine mansions reflecting the prosperity of textile yeomen in the 17th and 18th centuries. Such houses were built to accommodate both family home and business, and were always carefully sited. Greenwood Lee is on an old packhorse route from Heptonstall to Colne, and previously housed a waterwheel to provide power from local streams for the weaving machinery. The mullioned windows are found everywhere on old buildings in the region; their design allowed as much light as possible to enter the weaving chambers. Behind the chimneys in the picture, a line of treetops marks the edge of the Hardcastle Crags gorge. Beyond is Wadsworth Moor.

Blake Dean, Widdop, West Yorkshire. The uncompromising expanses of the South Pennine moors give way at their edges to steep valleys and sparkling streams. Many of these cloughs are remote and inaccessible, so it is no wonder that Blake Dean — on the treeline under Widdop Moor but also beside the Widdop road — is a favourite picnic spot. Two streams, Graining Water and Alcomden Water, meet here and continue as a single river through Hardcastle Crags and Hebden Bridge to the Calder. It is hard to imagine that this peaceful glade was once the site of a huge viaduct, 700ft long and 105ft high built on wooden trestles. At the turn of this century it carried a railway, complete with steam locomotives, that brought supplies from a point below Heptonstall to reservoir building sites high on the moor at Walshaw. Traces of the stone supports for the viaduct can still be found at Blake Dean, but in every other respect Nature has regained the upper hand.

The Piece Hall, Halifax, West Yorkshire. The Piece Hall is an architectural glory of the South Pennines and one of the great tourist successes of recent years. It was first opened in 1779 proclaiming Halifax's supremacy in the cloth trade. The Hall consists of a large open square surrounded by colonnades on two storeys where each of the 315 rooms was occupied by a cloth manufacturer. Smaller makers sold their cloth in the open area. During the 1970s the building was reopened and it now houses an industrial museum, restaurant, information centre and art gallery. Craftsmen and traders operate from the former merchants' rooms and there are regular open air markets and musical events in the quadrangle. The picture shows a spinning-wheel being demonstrated to prospective customers.

The Roman Road, Blackstone Edge, West Yorkshire. Located at 1,500ft above sea level at one of the highest points in the South Pennines, this paved track over Blackstone Edge between Rochdale and Halifax has long presented a headache to archaeologists and historians who dispute its origin. There is still much support for the theory that the exposed section of the causeway, dramatically sited just below the crest of the Edge facing West into Lancashire, is part of a Roman road. It has never been possible,

however, to establish the full extent of a route which would necessitate so arduous a climb up the face of Blackstone Edge when simple detours are quite practical. The troughed stones in the centre are also something of a mystery, and at 16–18ft wide the pavement is double the usual width for packhorse tracks. Perhaps the road was the first motorway — an early attempt to break the Pennine barrier like the M62 which runs just to the south. In any case travellers between Yorkshire and Lancashire have always

encountered problems crossing Blackstone Edge. Daniel Defoe (1724) gives a colourful account of his experience ascending the Edge in a snowstorm, but even earlier (1698) Celia Fiennes had recorded gloomily that it was 'noted all over England for a dismal high precipice . . . these high hills stagnate the air and hold mist and rains almost perpetually.'

New Bridge End Farm, near Trawden, Lancashire. This former hill farm under the edge of Red Spa Moor lies alongside the Nelson–Heptonstall road. In typical Pennine style, a stone wall careers up the steep hillside behind. Once a smallholding in its own right, the land has now been absorbed into a larger farm, but at least the building retains an agricultural function. Many small farmsteads are allowed to decay after purchase by the Water Authorities who operate a policy of moorland depopulation to conserve their water-gathering grounds. In this picture, taken in late autumn, sheep brought down from summer grazing on the open moor have been penned prior to release into enclosed pasture for the winter.

Wycoller Village, Lancashire. An old settlement of great beauty and seclusion Wycoller was originally an agricultural hamlet in the medieval Royal Forest of Trawden. It boasts no less than three examples of early bridges: an ancient clam bridge upstream of the present photograph; one of the best examples in England of a clapper bridge, itself perhaps 1,500 years old, seen in the foreground; and a double-arched packhorse bridge. The ruined Wycoller Hall on the right has a very grand window, restored fireplace and cockfighting pit, and is commonly supposed to have been the setting of Ferndean Manor in Charlotte Brontë's *Jane Eyre*. Wycoller was a busy handloom weaving community in the 17th century but was completely deserted after the coming of the Industrial Revolution. A proposal to flood the valley for a reservoir in the 1890s was fortunately dropped, and so, with the absence of a road through the village, Wycoller remained untouched. The area is now a Country Park and the restored houses in the village are newly inhabited.

Pendle Hill from pastures above Wycoller, Lancashire. Pendle Hill, once described as having its own supply of wind, is not officially a mountain at 1,831ft but has always been a landmark of great potency. Famous for the witches whose memory is exploited in gift shops for miles around, the hill is also a place of pilgrimage for Quakers. Their founder George Fox climbed Pendle in 1652 and had the vision which inspired his religious crusade. The view here from the edge of the Pennines shows Pendle rising strongly from the Lancashire plain. The unusual walls of upright stone slabs in the foreground are unique to the Wycoller area. Known as vaccary walls, their purpose was the winter enclosure of cattle in the large baronial vaccary farms of the Middle Ages, an attempt at economic agriculture which accompanied the felling of large areas of Royal Forest. The survival of these walls from the 11th and 12th centuries is another feature that makes the Wycoller district so fascinating.

Uppermill Museum, Saddleworth, Lancashire.
Uppermill is the largest of the villages which make up the Lancashire Pennine area called Saddleworth. Its museum contains a transport collection and local items recording the history of the woollen and cotton industries which thrived in the village during the Industrial Revolution. The museum building was itself part of a woollen mill, served by a wharf on the Huddersfield Narrow Canal which passes across the foreground of the picture. Opened in 1811 this canal is best-known for the 3¼-mile Standedge tunnel beneath the Pennines between Marsden and Diggle, one factor that inhibited its success compared to the Rochdale Canal which could also take wider boats. Nonetheless, records show that in the 1830s boats were leaving daily from the Saddleworth wharfs for London, Hull, Leeds, Goole, Wakefield, Manchester and Liverpool.

40

Healey Dell, near Rochdale, Lancashire. Lying just northwest of Rochdale, Healey Dell is a steep-sided clough formed by the action of the River Spodden. It boasts dramatic waterfalls and legends of fairies. The Dell is a local nature reserve with an exceptionally wide flora and fauna, but like Hardcastle Crags, 15 miles away, it also displays a long history of human occupation. This early spring view shows curious stone-arched footbridges which adjoin a now-ruined water-powered textile mill, itself built on the site of a Saxon cornmill. The prominent viaduct carried the former Rochdale-Bacup branch line. Now a footpath crosses the viaduct giving aerial perspectives of the surrounding woodland.

Gawthorpe Hall, Padiham, Lancashire. An Elizabethan hall built about 1600, Gawthorpe Hall was 'improved' in the 1850s by fashionable Gothic additions. It is situated beside the Lancashire Calder in verdant gardens, and houses important textile and furniture collections which are on view to the public. In 1850 Charlotte Brontë visited Gawthorpe at the insistence of its owner, Sir James Kay-Shuttleworth, who with his wife had sought out Charlotte in Haworth after the publication of *Shirley*. Charlotte stayed again with her husband, Arthur Nicholls, in 1855 when Sir James offered him the incumbency of Padiham church, an offer which was politely refused. Today the hall is owned by the National Trust and enjoys new life as a centre for craft studies.

Haworth Parsonage and Churchyard, West Yorkshire. Over 200,000 visitors pass annually through the Brontë Parsonage, here shown with its surroundings stripped bare by a heavy snowfall. The Georgian building dates from 1779 except for the tall gable end on the right which was added in 1872 by the Rev Patrick Brontë's successor who also rebuilt the church. Patrick Brontë brought his young family here in 1820, to a windswept moorland village whose population, prone to cholera and typhoid, had an average life expectancy of 26. One reason for this was the polluted water; one well actually rose within the churchyard where 40,000 people were said to have been buried by the time of its closure later in the century. Patrick Brontë himself agitated for a purer water supply, and the tall trees in the graveyard were planted partly to stabilise the ground and prevent the movement of graveyard waste down to the village below. The two fir trees standing in front of the Parsonage were planted by Charlotte Brontë and her husband Arthur Nicholls on their return from honeymoon in 1854.

Visitor pressure has not destroyed the powerful atmosphere of Haworth; the village has a hardiness which underlines the Brontë story, and which Emily, Charlotte, Anne and Branwell in their different ways absorbed.

Stanbury and Lower Laithe Reservoir from Penistone Hill, West Yorkshire. The descent to the Worth Valley from the Oxenhope road opens up a lovely panorama of the village strung along its ridge with moors stretching out all round and the reservoir below reflecting the sky. For a short time in late summer the immediate moorland blooms with purple: 'the brief flower-flush of August on the heather', Charlotte Brontë called it, thinking no doubt of the long winters which followed. The heather cover has diminished greatly in recent years, a result of pollution, the drying-up of the peat and over-grazing by sheep. Where it remains, the fragrance and colour chase away any thoughts of moorland harshness. And heather is not the only harvest — in early summer billberries can be found in profusion; even before that pockets of cottongrass make an early contrast with the moors' grey-green; and autumn produces more colour as rowan trees come into fruit and the bracken in the deep cloughs turns red-brown.

The Worth Valley and Stanbury Village, West Yorkshire. One of the earliest and best preserved examples of ribbon development, the village of Stanbury runs from west to east along the packhorse route connecting Bradford with Colne in Lancashire. It has seen little development in its long history, restricted as it is by the steep fields falling to either side of the ridge down to the Sladen and Worth Valleys. But the moors and fields surrounding it have seen much alteration. A hundred years ago there was a mill on the River Worth just below the village, the sides of the moor were liberally scattered with homesteads, and the decay and depopulation brought about by the construction of reservoirs and the closure of water-powered mills has only recently been halted with the arrival of a more mobile population in the 1970s. Stanbury has, for its size, more than its fair share of historical importance. It was the home of a group of early Quakers and a croft in the centre of the village, now marked by a stone plaque, was one of England's first Quaker graveyards. One of the early schoolmasters at the village school, Jonas Bradley, pioneered the teaching of nature study, giving every child his or her own plot of garden and taking the children out on to the moors. And Timmy Feather, a local character who died in 1910, was the last known handloom weaver. His weaving chamber is reconstructed in Cliffe Castle Museum in Keighley.

Field walls at Stanbury, under Haworth Moor, West Yorkshire.
A bold landscape of parallel gritstone walls, marching downhill from the edge of this moorland village, is picked out by the winter sun. The Enclosure Acts of the late 18th century altered the appearance of the Pennines by the building of dry stone walls up to and even across the highest moorland. Gangs of wallers worked across entire parishes creating the upland field patterns that we now consider 'natural'. With the retreat from the cultivation of marginal land and the breaking-up of smallholdings into larger farms, miles of these walls are now redundant, a fact which accounts for the derelict appearance of many moorland fringes. Walling is now so expensive that ony essential walls can be economically repaired.

Hill Farms, Upper Worth Valley, West Yorkshire. On the horizon can be seen the water-tower of Watersheddles Reservoir, at the head of the Worth Valley, on the Lancashire border. An old packhorse road from Colne and Wycoller led past the two nearer farms towards Stanbury and Haworth before the building of the modern road down on the valley floor. Old Snap (the distant of these two farms) was the seat of the Heaton family who later built Ponden Hall. It was their library, reputed to contain a first folio of Shakespeare and other literary gems, to which Emily Brontë had access at Ponden Hall. Certain details of the family background were also known to her, and in all probability inspired much of the plot of *Wuthering Heights*. Whitestone Farm in the foreground was another Heaton farm. In both dwellings the typical lines of the Pennine longhouse are evident — a small living area continuing into a larger barn where animals and crops were housed

The Courtyard, Skipton Castle, North Yorkshire. The market town of Skipton marks the northern boundary of the South Pennines and the beginning of the Dales. Overlooking the town stands its Norman castle, partially dismantled by Cromwell after a three-year siege by Parliamentary forces during the Civil War, but rebuilt to an imposing standard by Lady Anne Clifford after the Restoration. At the heart of the castle is the elevated courtyard we see here, from which the rooms lead on three storeys. Lady Anne planted the yew tree which now quite fills the courtyard, but the graceful architecture of the walls is original Tudor. In no sense a ruin, although mostly unfurnished, Skipton Castle has a unique atmosphere which seems to communicate a real sense of how life there might have been lived.

The Five-Rise Locks, Bingley, West Yorkshire. The Leeds & Liverpool was the last trans-Pennine canal to be completed (1816) and at 127 miles it is the longest canal in Britain. Unlike the Rochdale Canal to the south it has remained open and is now heavily used by holidaymakers. From Leeds the canal keeps close to the River Aire, but at Bingley two sets of locks, first a three-rise and then a staircase of five take the canal 90ft up the valley side, not to rejoin the river till the far side of Skipton. Beautifully maintained, the five-rise is in almost constant use during the summer weeks, although passage through it is remarkably quick.

Saltaire. The 'planned' industrial township of Saltaire is a great example of Victorian paternalism. It was built by Sir Titus Salt, a leading Bradford industrialist, between 1851 and 1871 as a model community around his mill on the banks of the River Aire. Saltaire included a large library and town hall, a hospital, a school and a spacious park — but no public houses. The picture is taken from the steps of the round-fronted Roman classical style Congregational Church, looking towards the Mill with its campanile chimney copied from a Venetian church. Still open, the Mill in its heyday employed 3,000 people who lived in terraced houses along the geometrically laid out streets, each of which bears the name of a member of the Salt family.

East Riddlesden Hall, Keighley, West Yorkshire. Standing on ground above the River Aire which has been inhabited since the earliest times, the present East Riddlesden Hall was built by a wealthy clothier James Murgatroyd in the mid-17th century. The two-storey entrance porch is only one of many splendid architectural features which combine Gothic and classical styles. In the grounds are a fishpond fished by the Canons of Bolton in the 14th century and a huge timbered barn, one of the finest in the north. The house and pond both have tales of hauntings connected with a number of murders and accidental deaths which have occurred within the gates. The shortest visit to this National Trust house — now incongruously surrounded by ribbon development along the Keighley-Bradford road — produces a powerful sense of its mysterious past. At dusk the impression is even stronger.

BIBLIOGRAPHY

The cohesion of the South Pennines as a distinct area has only recently been recognised, and the 'standard works' on the region have probably still to be written. Much of the available information is to be found in local pamphlets and guidebooks, best obtained from the well-stocked information centres at Hebden Bridge and Haworth.

Much work is currently being done by Pennine Heritage, an organisation in Hebden Bridge dedicated to the cultural and economic renewal of the South Pennines, to provide basic information in printed form. There is a bi-monthly *Pennine Magazine*, and the Pennine Heritage Network publish a series of booklets on man and the landscape, transport, textiles and social history. In particular we have consulted two booklets in the transport series which both contain original material:

Early Trackways by Margaret & David Drake
Turnpikes & Canals by Mary Johnston & Clive Whitehead.

Publications from other sources are listed below:

The Making of the Central Pennines, John Porter, Moorland Publishing Co, 1980
Trans-Pennine Heritage, Keith Parry, David & Charles, 1981
South Pennine Park, Herbert C. Collins, Dalesman Books 1974
Wayfarer Walks in the South Pennines, Colin Speakman, Dalesman Books 1982
Hebden Bridge Official Guide, Metro Publishing, 1983
Portrait of Lancashire, Jessica Lofthouse, Robert Hale 1967

The Brontës

Haworth & The Brontës, W. R. Mitchell, Dalesman Books, 1983
The Life of Charlotte Brontë, Mrs Gaskell
Charlotte Brontë, Winifred Gérin, Oxford University Press, 1967
Emily Brontë, Winifred Gérin, Oxford University Press, 1971

Collections of photographs

Remains of Elmet, Fay Godwin & Ted Hughes, Faber, 1979
Pennine Landscapes, Simon & Judith Warner, Dalesman Books, 1979

Maps

Ordnance Survey 1:25,000 Outdoor Leisure Series, *South Pennines*
Pennine Heritage Network Geology Map and Wallchart, *How the South Pennines were made.*